Hamilton Beach Indoor Grill Cookbook for Beginners

Tasty and Unique Recipes for Indoor Grilling Perfection (Less Smoke, Less Mess, More Flavor)

Ilane Swanmart

Table of Contents

Introduction

There's nothing like the smell of freshly grilled steak. The enticing and inviting aroma in the air around you, the sizzling when the meat touches the hot plate, the blackened seared lines you enjoy so much. But when the weather turns against you, it is hard to plan a grilling day in the backyard. But how about your home?

With the Hamilton Beach Indoor Grill, you can have it all – freshly grilled specialties in the comfort of your own home. Away from the rain, wind, or hot sun, with the indoor grill, there is no guesswork involved. Just follow the grill instructions, and delights are guaranteed.

And this cookbook is created to give you just that. 70 mouthwatering recipes you can make on your indoor grill. Whether looking for a meal for breakfast, snack, side dish, dinner, or even dessert (pretty cool, right?), we've got you covered.

And with the ultimate tips on how to use the MultiGrill included, it is safe to say that this cookbook is the only indoor grilling guide you will ever need. Read on and see for yourself!

Chapter 1: Hamilton Beach Indoor MultiGrill Basics

So you've bought yourself a shiny new indoor grill. Congratulations! Once you get the handle of it, you can create anything from eggs for breakfast and juicy steaks for dinner to delightful sweet bites to finish off your meals. Luckily for you, this chapter will help you learn all there is to know about using the Hamilton Beach Indoor Grill.

Why Do You Need It?

There are a lot of reasons why your house needs this HB indoor grill. And if you don't already have one sitting in this kitchen, hopefully, the benefits below will encourage you to hit the stores and purchase one today.

Large Nonstick Cooking Surface...

The Hamilton Beach 3-in-1 MultiGrill has a large surface to cook on – 100 square inch, to be precise. So, cooking for a crowd is a breeze with this appliance. Being able to prepare a decent amount of food in a very short time makes this indoor grill incredibly appealing.

And the fact that your meat will not stick to it is an added plus, for sure.

Which You Can Actually Double

That's right; you can actually open the grill flat, doubling the cooking surface. So, instead of the amazing 100 square inches, you can get mind-blowing 200 square inches of grilling area.

Quicker Cooking

Thanks to the double cooking grates, you can simply arrange your food onto the bottom plate, lower the lid, and cut the cooking time in half without having to flip over your ingredients. How great is that?

Three Cooking Modes

There is a good reason why this appliance is wearing the "3-in-1 Grill" name proudly. Because you can grill, griddle, and cook bacon on it.

1. The Grill Mode – Allows you to cook your meats perfectly
2. The Griddle Mode – Is perfect for your eggs and morning pancakes
3. The Bacon Mode – Will help you get the crispiest strips of bacon ever.

Adjustable Temperature

If you're all about customizing your meals, then you'll love the fact that this grill allows you to adjust your temperature so you can get the perfect degree of cooking. Besides, this feature also ensures that the food is always cooked evenly, whether on low or high, which is another benefit.

Plus, with the indicator light, you can always know whether it's safe for you to touch the grill or pinpoint the perfect time to place your food onto the plate.

Perfect Drainage

If you enjoy the greasy (and guilty) pleasures, you might be worried about the excess grease dripping from all sides. Well, that may be the case with other indoor grills (or microwaving bacon), but the Hamilton Beach Indoor MultiGrill has come with a perfect solution. Thanks to their perfectly designed kickstand, you will never have to worry about fatty drips.

Crispy bacon with no mess is guaranteed with the HB Indoor 3-in-1 Grill.

Splatter-Free Cooking

Besides perfect drainage and grease-free cooking, you can actually enjoy cooking more with this appliance, thanks to the fact that there is no splattering involved. Because, in most cases, the lid will be lowered when cooking, you can say goodbye to annoying splatters while searing your dinner steak.

Using the Hamilton Beach 3-in-1 MultiGrill

Being a three-in-one kind of appliance may trick you into thinking that this grill is overwhelming to use, but once you plug it in and start cooking, you will see that it is not only very straightforward, but it also doesn't require particular grilling skills, either.

Just follow our step-by-step instructions, and you're good to go.

Grilling

First of all, make sure always to use oven mittens for safety and protection when grilling. Start by aligning the tabs of the grill plates with their openings. Press well until you hear the clicking sound, which indicates that everything is into place. The drip tray should be slided in.

1. Plug the device in. The red indicator light should be on.
2. Set the desired temperature (250 to 400 degrees F) to preheat the grill.
3. When preheated, the green indicator light will turn on. At this point, you can place the food onto the plate for grilling.
4. Depending on the method of cooking, you may lower the grill lid if desired.
5. Lift the lid halfway through to check the food. If done, transfer to a plate.
6. Unplug the device and let it cool completely before cleaning the grill. Make sure not to touch the tray until it is completely cool.

Using the Griddle

Just like with grilling, it is highly recommended you use oven mittens when using the griddle, as well.

1. Plug the device in and make sure that the drip tray is in place. If you need a larger cooking surface, open the unit. Keep in mind, though, that that will require more time to cook and turning the food over halfway through.
2. Adjust the preferred temperature and wait for the green light to turn on.
3. When preheated, open the locked hinge as far as it goes, and lay it on your working surface.
4. Arrange the food on top of the griddle and start cooking.
5. Halfway through, flip over to ensure even cooking.
6. Transfer to a plate and unplug the appliance. Wait until it is completely cool to clean, and do not touch until cool enough to handle.

Cooking Bacon

If you depend on your crispy bacon for breakfast, then cooking it on the HB 3-in-1 grill will be your go-to method.

1. First, you will need to make sure that the kickstand is in position, as it is important for draining the bacon grease away. You can do this by lifting the back of the unit and rotating the kickstand. That should put it in place.
2. Plug the unit in.
3. For best (and crispiest) results, preheat the grill to 400 degrees F, keeping the unit closed in the meantime. Wait for the green indicator light to turn on.
4. Once preheated, open the lid and arrange the bacon onto the bottom plate.
5. Lower the lid and let the bacon cook. Normal bacon slices usually take between 7 to 10 minutes to become super crispy. You can cook it with the lid open as well, but keep in mind that keeping it closed will allow splatter-free cooking and even crispiness.
6. Once the desired doneness is reached, lift the cover and grab some plastic utensils to transfer the bacon to a serving plate.
7. Unplug the grill and let it sit until cool enough to handle. Do not try to clean until completely cool.

Cleaning the Appliance

Before you even attempt to clean the appliance, make sure that you:

- Unplug the appliance first
- Wait until the grill is completely safe to handle
- Never immerse the cord, base, and plug into liquid
- Never clean with abrasive cleaners
- Do not use metal utensils as they can seriously damage the nonstick coat on the surface

Once you make sure that you handle with safety and caution, follow these steps:

1. Unplug the device.
2. Push the button that releases the upper plate of the grill. Remove it and set aside. Do the same with the bottom plate. Press release and set it aside.
3. Check the condition of the grill. Sometimes grease finds its way under the top and bottom plates. If not completely clean, grab a soapy sponge and gently wipe the

surface. Then, with a damp cloth, wipe again. Grab a clean towel (or kitchen towels) and pat dry.

4. Clean the outside of the unit, as well. Simply wipe with a damp cloth and then wipe it dry afterward.

5. Now, it is time to tackle the actual plates. You can clean them with a soft sponge drenched in warm, soapy water. Rinse under clean water, and then let dry completely before locking them back into place. And if this sounds easy, wait until you hear that they are all dishwasher safe. If you have a dishwashing machine in your kitchen, you can simply pop them in, and voila.

Troubleshooting and Fixing Common Issues

Although this is truly a unit of high quality, we shouldn't forget that there is nothing magical about it. It is an electric appliance, after all, and just like with any devices, when using the HB indoor grill, you may bump into some obstacles occasionally.

But don't fret! We have compiled this section to make your life easier. Below, you will find the common issues users face when handling this indoor grill, and learn how to fix them, easily.

The Device Won't Start. Check if the grill is actually plugged in. If it is but still cannot start, check your power outlet - maybe the issue is not in the unit at all. You can also check the breaker box to make sure power is working.

Remember, when plugged in, the indicator light will turn on.

The Grease Is Not Draining. If you have grease dripping, and not draining, there are two possible reasons for it. The first one is that your kickstand is not locked in place. Grab some oven mittens and check if it is sitting correctly – reassemble if needed.

The second reason may occur if you haven't cleaned under the plates for some time. If not maintained regularly, the drain hole may get clogged. Unplug the unit and let cool completely, then clean around the drain hole well, to get rid of leftover gunk.

The Grill Overcooks. If your food is overcooked, then it is not the grill's fault at all. Try to lower the temperature or cut the cooking time shorter. For meat, you can invest in a good thermostat that will measure the internal temperature so you can know precisely when the food is cooked.

The Grill Undercooks. If your food is undercooked, obviously, the reason can be not enough cooking time or temperature. Try to cook longer and increase the heat if that is the issue. However, the grill can undercook your food if the plates are not placed correctly. Check the top and bottom plate and see if they are pressed into place.

For best results, allow the grill to fully preheat before adding food to it, and cook with the lid lowered.

Chapter 2: Breakfast Recipes

Classic Bacon and Eggs Breakfast

Preparation Time: 2 minutes
Cooking Time: 8 minutes
Servings: 1

Ingredients:

- 2 Eggs
- 2 Bacon Slices
- 2 Bread Slices
- Salt and Pepper, to taste

Method:

1. Preheat your grill to 400 degrees F, and make sure that the kickstand is in position.
2. When the light goes on, add the bacon to the plate and lower the lid.
3. Let cook for 4 full minutes.
4. Open the lid and crack the eggs onto the plate. Season with salt and pepper.
5. Add the bread slices to the plate, as well.
6. Cook for 4 minutes, turning the bread and bacon (and the eggs if you desire) over ha-lfway through.
7. Transfer carefully to a plate. Enjoy!

Nutritional Value:

- Calories 434
- Total Fats 19.6g
- Carbs 38.8g
- Protein 25.6g
- Fiber: 6g

Quick Oat & Banana Pancakes

Preparation Time: 8 minutes
Cooking Time: 5 minutes
Servings: 4

Ingredients:

- ½ cup Oats
- ¼ cup chopped Nuts by choice (Walnuts and Hazelnuts work best)
- 1 large Ripe Banana, chopped finely
- 2 cups Pancake Mix

Method:

1. Preheat your grill to medium and unlock the hinge. Open it flat on your counter.
2. Meanwhile, prepare the pancake mix according to the instruction on the package.
3. Stir in the remaining ingredients well.
4. Spray the griddle with some cooking spray.
5. Drop about ¼ cup onto the griddle.
6. Cook for a minute or two, just until the pancake begins to puff up.
7. Flip over and cook for another minute or so – the recipe makes about 16 pancakes.
8. Serve as desired and enjoy!

Nutritional Value:

- Calories 310
- Total Fats 8g
- Carbs 56g
- Protein 14g
- Fiber: 8g

Sausage and Mushroom Breakfast Skewers

Preparation Time: 8-10 minutes
Cooking Time: 4 minutes
Servings: 4

Ingredients:

- 2 Italian Sausage Links
- 4 Whole White Button Mushrooms
- 1 Red Bell Pepper
- Salt and Pepper, to taste

Method:

1. Soak four skewers in cold water for 2-3 minutes.
2. Preheat your grill to 375 degrees F.
3. Meanwhile, cut each sausage in eight pieces.
4. Quarter the mushrooms and cut the red pepper into eight pieces.
5. Sprinkle the mushrooms and pepper generously with salt and pepper.
6. Grab the skewers and thread the ingredients – sausage, mushroom, pepper, sausage mushroom, sausage mushroom, pepper, sausage, mushroom, in that order.
7. Place onto the grill and lower the lid.
8. Cook for 4 minutes closed.
9. Serve alongside some bread and a favorite spread and enjoy.

Nutritional Value:

- Calories 118
- Total Fats 9.1g
- Carbs 4g
- Protein 7.3g
- Fiber: 0.6g

Corn Cakes with Salsa and Cream Cheese

Preparation Time: 8 minutes
Cooking Time: 8 minutes
Servings: 8

Ingredients:

- ½ cup Cornmeal
- ¼ cup Butter, melted
- ½ cup Salsa
- 14 ounces canned Corn, drained
- 1 cup Milk
- 6 ounces Cream Cheese
- 1 ½ cups Flour
- 6 Eggs
- ¼ cup chopped Spring Onions
- 1 tsp Baking Powder
- Salt and Pepper, to taste

Method:

1. In a bowl, whisk together the eggs, butter, cream cheese, and milk.
2. Whisk in the cornmeal, flour, baking powder, salt, and pepper.
3. Fold in the remaining ingredients and stir well to incorporate.
4. Preheat your grill to medium.
5. When the light is on, unlock the hinge and lower to your counter.
6. Spray the griddle with a nonstick spray.
7. Ladle the batter onto the griddle (about ¼ of cup per cake).
8. When the cakes start bubbling, flip them over and cook until golden brown.
9. Serve as desired and enjoy!

Nutritional Value:

- Calories 325

- Total Fats 15g
- Carbs 35g
- Protein 11g
- Fiber: 3g

Mexican Eggs on Haystacks

Preparation Time: 10 minutes
Cooking Time: 12 minutes
Servings: 6

Ingredients:

- ½ cup Breadcrumbs
- 3 ½ cups Store-Bought Hash Browns
- 2/3 cup Sour Cream
- 2 tsp Tex Mex Seasoning
- 6 Eggs
- 1/3 cup shredded Cheddar
- Salt and Pepper, to taste

Method:

1. Preheat your grill to medium.
2. In the meantime, squeeze the hash browns to get rid of excess water, and place in a bowl.
3. Add the breadcrumbs, cheese, half of the Tex-Mex, and season with some salt and pepper.
4. Mix with your hands to combine.
5. Open the grill, unlock the hinge for the griddle, and lay it open. Spray with cooking spray.
6. Make six patties out of the hash brown mixture and arrange onto the griddle.
7. Cook for 7 minutes, flipping once, halfway through. Tarsnsfer to six serving plates.
8. Crack the eggs open onto the griddle, season with salt and pepper, and cook until they reach your preferred consistency.
9. Top the hash browns with the egg.
10. Combine the sourcream and remaining Tex Mex and top the eggs with it.
11. Enjoy!

Nutritional Value:

- Calories 340
- Total Fats 21g
- Carbs 25g
- Protein 8.2g
- Fiber: 2g

Chocolate Chip and Blueberry Pancakes

Preparation Time: 5 minutes
Cooking Time: 5 minutes
Servings: 2

Ingredients:

- 1 cup Pancake Mix
- ¼ cup Orange Juice
- 1/3 cup Fresh Blueberries
- ¼ cup Chocolate Chips
- ½ cup Water

Method:

1. Preheat your grill to medium.
2. Meanwhile, combine the pancake mix with the orange juice and water.
3. Fold in the chocolate chips and blueberries.
4. Open the grill, unhinge, and lay the griddle onto your counter.
5. Spray with cooking spray.
6. Add about 1/6 of the batter at a time, to the griddle.
7. Cook until bubbles start forming on the surface, then flip over, and cook until the other side turns golden brown.
8. Serve and enjoy!

Nutritional Value:

- Calories 370
- Total Fats 9g
- Carbs 66g
- Protein 3g
- Fiber: 3g

Grilled Ham Omelet

Preparation Time: 5 minutes
Cooking Time: 5 minutes
Servings: 2

Ingredients:

- 6 Eggs
- 2 Ham Slices, chopped
- 2 tbsp chopped Herbs by choice
- ¼ tsp Onion Powder
- 1 tbsp minced Red Pepper
- ¼ tsp Garlic Powder
- Salt and Pepper, to taste

Method:

1. Preheat your grill to 350 degrees F.
2. In the meantime, whisk the eggs in a bowl and add the rest of the ingredients to it. Stir well to combine.
3. Open the grill and unlock the hinge.
4. Coat the griddle with some cooking spray and gently pour the egg mixture onto it.
5. With a silicone spatula, mix the omelet as you would in a skillet.
6. When it reaches your desired consistency, divide among two serving plates.
7. Enjoy!

Nutritional Value:

- Calories 271
- Total Fats 17.5g
- Carbs 2.4g
- Protein 24g
- Fiber: 0.1g

Chapter 3: Beef and Pork Recipes

Pork Burnt Ends

Preparation Time: 10 minutes

Cooking Time: 6 minutes

Servings: 1

Ingredients:

- 1-pound Pork Shoulder
- 2 tbsp Favorite Rub Spice
- 2 tbsp Honey
- 1 ½ tbsp Barbecue Sauce

Method:

1. Start by chopping the pork into cubes.
2. Place the meat in a bowl and add the spice, honey, and barbecue sauce.
3. With your hands, mix wel, making sure that each meat cube gets a little bit of honey, sauce, and spices.
4. Preheat your grill to 375 degrees F.
5. Arange the pork onto the bottom plate and lower the lid.
6. Cook for about 6 minutes.
7. Check the meat – if it is not too burnt for your taste, cook for an additional minute.
8. Serve as desired.
9. Enjoy!

Nutritional Value:

- Calories 399
- Total Fats 27g
- Carbs 10.8g
- Protein 27g

- Fiber: 0g

Steak Skewers with Potatoes and Mushrooms

Preparation Time: 35 minutes

Cooking Time: 10 minutes

Servings: 6

Ingredients:

- 1-pound Steak
- 4 tbsp Olive Oil
- ½ pound Button Mushrooms
- 4 tbsp Balsamic Vinegar
- 1 pound Very Small Potatoes, boiled
- 2 tsp minced Garlic
- ½ tsp dired Sage
- Salt and Pepper, to taste

Method:

1. Start by cutting the steak into 1-inch pieces.
2. Quarter the mushrooms.
3. Whisk the vinegar, oil, garlic, sage, and salt and pepper, in a bowl.
4. Add the meat, murshooms and potatoes to the bowl, coat well, and place in the fridge for 30 minutes. If your potatoes are not small enough for the skewers, you can chop them into smaller chunks.
5. In the meantime, soak the skewers in cold water.
6. Meanwhile, preheat your grill to medium-high.
7. Thread the chunks onto the skewers and arrange them on the bottom plate.
8. Keep the lid open and cook for 5.
9. Flip over and cook for 5 more minutes.
10. Serve and enjoy!

Nutritional Value:

- Calories 383

- Total Fats 23g
- Carbs 21g
- Protein 23g
- Fiber: 3g

Chipotle BBQ Ribs

Preparation Time: 5 minutes

Cooking Time: 16 minutes

Servings: 4

Ingredients:

- 1-pound Back Ribs
- 3 tbsp Brown Sugar
- 1 ¾ cups BBQ Sauce
- 2/3 cups Balsamic Vinegar
- ½ tsp Chipotle Pepper
- ¼ tsp Garlic Powder
- Salt and Pepper, to taste

Method:

1. Preheat your grill to 325 degrees F.
2. Sprinkle the ribs with salt, pepper, and garlic powder, and place on the bottom plate of the grill.
3. Cook for 8 minutes with the lid lowered.
4. In the meantime, combine the balsamic, BBQ sauce, sugar, and chipotle.
5. Lift the lid and sprinkle the mixture over the ribs.
6. Cook uncovered for about 8 more minutes, occasionally flipping over and adding more sauce as needed.
7. Serve and enjoy!

Nutritional Value:

- Calories 400
- Total Fats 9g
- Carbs 75g
- Protein 7g
- Fiber: 1g

Maple Pork Chops

Preparation Time: 65 minutes
Cooking Time: 7-8 minutes
Servings: 1

Ingredients:

- 4 boneless Pork Chops
- 6 tbsp Balsamic Vinegar
- 6 tbsp Maple Syrup
- ¼ tsp ground Sage
- Salt and Pepper, to taste

Method:

1. Whisk the vinegar, maple, sage, and some salt and pepper in a bowl.
2. Add the pork chops and coat well.
3. Cover with plastic foil and refrigerate for one hour.
4. Preheat your grill to 350 degrees F.
5. Open and arrange the chops onto the bottom plate.
6. Lower the lid and cook closed for about 7 minutes, or until your desired doneness is reached.
7. Serve and enjoy!

Nutritional Value:

- Calories 509
- Total Fats 19g
- Carbs 15g
- Protein 65g
- Fiber: 0g

Garlicky Marinated Steak

Preparation Time: 2 minutes
Cooking Time: 8 minutes
Servings: 1

Ingredients:

- 4 Steaks (about 1 - 1 ½ pounds)
- 3 tbsp minced Garlic
- ¼ cup Soy Sauce
- 2 tbsp Honey
- ¼ cup Balsamic Vinegar
- 2 tbsp Worcesteshire Sauce
- ½ tsp Onion Powder
- Salt and Pepper, to taste

Method:

1. Whisk together the garlic, sauces, and spices, in a bowl.
2. Add the steaks to it and make sure to coat them well.
3. Cover with plastic foil and refrigerate for about an hour.
4. Preheat your grill to high.
5. Open and add your steaks to the bottom plate.
6. Lower the lid and cook for about 4 minutes, or until the meat reaches the internal temperature that you prefer.
7. Serve as desired and let sit for a couple of minutes before enjoying!

Nutritional Value:

- Calories 435
- Total Fats 24g
- Carbs 19g
- Protein 37g
- Fiber: 1g

Herbed Lemony Pork Skewers

Preparation Time: 10 minutes
Cooking Time: 8 minutes
Servings: 4

Ingredients:

- 1-pound Pork Shoulder or Neck
- 1 tsp dried Basil
- 1 tsp dried Parsley
- 1 tsp dried Oregano
- 2 Garlic Cloves, minced
- 4 tbsp Lemon Juice
- ¼ tsp Onion Powder
- Salt and Pepper, to taste

Method:

1. Start by soaking 8 skewers in cold water, to prevent the wood from burning on the grill.
2. Cut the pork into small chunks and place in a bowl.
3. Add lemon juice, garlic, spices and herbs to the bowl.
4. Give the mixture a good stir so that the meat is coated well.
5. Preheat your grill to medium-high.
6. Meanwhile, thread the meat onto the skewers.
7. When the green light turns on, arrange the skewers onto the bottom plate.
8. Cook for about 4 minutes per side (or more if you like the meat well-done and almost burnt).
9. Serve as desired and enjoy!

Nutritional Value:

- Calories 364
- Total Fats 27g

- Carbs 1.6g
- Protein 26.7g
- Fiber: 0.1g

Hawaian Kebobs

Preparation Time: 70 minutes
Cooking Time: 6 minutes
Servings: 4

Ingredients:

- ½ cup Orange Juice
- 1 tbsp minced Garlic
- 1/3 cup Brown Sugar
- ½ tbs minced Ginger
- ½ cup Soy Sauce
- 1-pound Top Sirloin
- 1-pound Pineapple, fresh
- 2 Bell Peppers
- ½ Red Onion

Method:

1. Place the first 5 ingredients in a medium bowl. Whisk to combine well.
2. Cut the steak into pieces and add to the bowl.
3. Stir well to coat, cover with plastic wrap, and place in the fridge for at least 60 minutes.
4. Meanwhile, cut the red onion, pineapple, and bell pepper, into chunks.
5. If using wooden skewers, soak them in cold water.
6. Preheat your grill to medium-high.
7. Thread the steak, pineapple, onion, and bell peppers onto the skewers.
8. Open the grill and arrange the skewers onto the bottom plate.
9. Cover, and let cook for 6 minutes.
10. Serve and enjoy!

Nutritional Value:

- Calories 460

- Total Fats 13g
- Carbs 51g
- Protein 33g
- Fiber: 0.7g

Chapter 4: Poultry Recipes

Chicken Yakitori

Preparation Time: 70 minutes

Cooking Time: 6 minutes

Servings: 4

Ingredients:

- 2 tbsp Honey
- 1 tsp minced Garlic
- 1-pound boneless Chicken
- 1 tsp minced Ginger
- 4 tbsp Soy Sauce
- Salt and Pepper, to taste

Method:

1. In a bowl, combine the honey, ginger, soy sauce, and garlic. Add some salt and pepper.
2. Cut the chicken into thick stripes and add them to the bowl.
3. Mix until the meat is completely coated with the marinade.
4. Cover the bowl and refrigerate for about one hour.
5. Preheat your grill to medium.
6. Thread the chicken onto metal (or soaked wooden) skewers and arrange onto the bottom plate.
7. Lower the lid and cook for about 6-7 minutes, depending on how well-cooked you prefer the meat to be.
8. Serve and enjoy!

Nutritional Value:

- Calories 182
- Total Fats 9g

- Carbs 10g
- Protein 27g
- Fiber: 0.2g

Basil Grilled Chicken with Asparagus

Preparation Time: 15 minutes
Cooking Time: 7 minutes
Servings: 4

Ingredients:

- 1 tsp Dijon Mustard
- 1 pound boneless and skinless Chicken Breasts
- 1 tsp dried Basil
- 1 tsp minced Garlic
- 2 tbsp Olive Oil
- ¼ tsp Onion Powder
- 12 Asparagus Spears
- Salt and Pepper, to taste

Method:

1. Combine the oil, mustard, basil, garlic, onion powder, and some salt and pepper, in a bowl.
2. Coat the chicken with this mixture.
3. Meanwhile, preheat your grill to 350 degrees F.
4. Arrange the chicken breasts onto the bottom plate.
5. Season the asparagus with salt and pepper and add them next to the chicken.
6. Lower the lid, and cook closed, for 7 full minutes, or until your preferred doneness is reached.
7. Serve and enjoy!

Nutritional Value:

- Calories 350
- Total Fats 24g
- Carbs 6g
- Protein 26g
- Fiber: 2g

Lemon and Rosemary Turkey and Zucchini Threads

Preparation Time: 70 minutes

Cooking Time: 7 minutes

Servings: 4

Ingredients:

- 1-pound Turkey Breasts, boneless and skinless
- 1 Large Zuchinni
- 2 tbsp Lemon Juice
- ½ tsp Lemon Zest
- ¼ cup Olive Oil
- 1 tbsp Honey
- 1 tbsp Fresh Rosemary
- ¼ tsp Garlic Powder
- Salt and Pepper, to taste

Method:

1. Cut the Turkey into smaller chunks, and place inside a bowl.
2. Add the olive oil, lemon juice, zest, honey, rosemary, garlic powder, and some salt and pepper, to the bowl.
3. With your hands, mix well until the turkey is completely coated with the mixture.
4. Cover and let sit in the fridge for about an hour.
5. Wash the zucchini thoroughly and cut into small chunks. Season with salt and pepper.
6. Preheat your Grill to 350 – 375 degrees F.
7. Thread the turkey and zucchini onto soaked (or metal) skewers and arrange on the bottom plate.
8. Lower the lid and cook closed for 6-7 minutes.
9. Serve and enjoy!

Nutritional Value:

- Calories 280
- Total Fats 23g
- Carbs 6g
- Protein 27g
- Fiber: 0.5g

Whiskey Wings

Preparation Time: 10 minutes
Cooking Time: 6 minutes
Servings: 4

Ingredients:

- 1 tbsp Whiskey
- 1/2 tbsp Chili Powder
- 1 tsp Paprika
- 20 Chicken Wings
- ¼ tsp Garlic Powder
- Salt and Pepper, to taste
- 2 tsp Brown Sugar

Method:

1. Preheat your grill to 375 degrees F.
2. In the meantime, dump all of the ingredients in a large bowl.
3. With your hands, mix well, to coat the chicken wings completely.
4. When the green light is on, open the grill and arrange the chicken wings onto it.
5. Lower the lid and cook closed for 6 minutes. You can check near the end to see if you need to increase (or decrease) the grilling time for your preferred doneness.
6. Serve with rice and enjoy!

Nutritional Value:

- Calories 210
- Total Fats 21g
- Carbs 9.3g
- Protein 18g
- Fiber: 0g

Duck Veggie Kebobs

Preparation Time: 15 minutes
Cooking Time: 7 minutes
Servings: 2

Ingredients:

- 8 ounces boneless and skinless Duck (breast is fine)
- 1/2 small Squash
- ½ Zucchini
- 1 small Red Bell Pepper
- ¼ Red Onion
- 2 tbsp Olive Oil
- 1 tbsp Balsamic Vinegar
- 2 tsp Dijon Mustard
- 2 tsp Honey
- Salt and Pepper, to taste

Method:

1. Whisk together the oil, vinegar, mustard, honey, and some salt and pepper, in a bowl.
2. Cut the duck into chunks and dump into the bowl.
3. Mix to coat well and set aside. You can leave in the fridge for an hour or two, but if you are in a hurry, you can place on the grill straight away – it will taste great, as well.
4. Cut the veggies into chunks.
5. Plug the grill in, and set the temperature to 375 degrees F.
6. Thread the duck and veggies onto metallic skewers.
7. Open the grill and place on the bottom plate.
8. Lower the lid and cook for 5-8 minutes, depending on how *done* you want the meat to be.
9. Serve and enjoy!

Nutritional Value:

- Calories 250
- Total Fats 10g
- Carbs 11g
- Protein 30g
- Fiber: 2g

Teriyaki Chicken Thighs

Preparation Time: 70 minutes
Cooking Time: 7 minutes
Servings: 4

Ingredients:

- 4 Chicken Thighs
- ½ cup Brown Sugar
- ½ cup Teriyaki Sauce
- 2 tbsp Rice Vinegar
- 1 thumb-sized piece of Ginger, minced
- ¼ cup Water
- 2 tsp minced Garlic
- 1 tbsp Cornstarch

Method:

1. Place the sugar, teriyaki sauce, vinegar, ginger, water, and garlic, in a bowl.
2. Mix to combine well.
3. Transfer half of the mixture to a saucepan and set aside.
4. Add the chicken thighs to the bowl, and coat well.
5. Cover the bowl with wrap, and place in the fridge. Let sit for one hour.
6. Preheat your grill to medium.
7. In the meantime, place the saucepan over medium heat and add the cornstarch. Cook until thickened. Remove from heat and set aside.
8. Arrange the thighs onto the preheated bottom and close the lid.
9. Cook for 5 minutes, then open, brush the thickened sauce over, and cover again.
10. Cook for additional minute or two.
11. Serve and enjoy!

Nutritional Value:

- Calories 321

- Total Fats 11g
- Carbs 28g
- Protein 31g
- Fiber: 1g

Simple Cajun Chicken Legs

Preparation Time: 2 minutes

Cooking Time: 8 minutes

Servings: 1

Ingredients:

- 8 Chicken Legs, boneless
- 2 tbsp Olive Oil
- 2 tbsp Cajun Seasoning

Method:

1. Preheat your grill to medium-high.
2. Brush them with the olive oil, and then rub the legs with the seasoning.
3. When the green light is on, arrange the legs onto the bottom plate.
4. Lower the lid, and let the legs cook closed, for about 8 to 10 minutes.
5. Serve with the favorite side dish, Enjoy!

Nutritional Value:

- Calories 370
- Total Fats 19.2g
- Carbs 0.5g
- Protein 35g
- Fiber: 0g

Chapter 5: Fish & Seafood Recipes

Lime Sea Bass

Preparation Time: 5 minutes
Cooking Time: 9 minutes
Servings: 4

Ingredients:

- ½ tsp Garlic Powder
- 4 tbsp Lime Juice
- 4 Sea Bass Fillets
- Salt and Pepper, to taste

Method:

1. Preheat your grill to 375 degrees F.
2. Brush the fillets with lime juice and sprinkle with garlic powder, salt, and pepper.
3. When the green light is on, open the grill, coat with cooking spray, and arrange the fillets on top.
4. Cook open for 4 minutes. Then flip over and cook for 4-5 more minutes on the other side.
5. Serve with rice or favorite side dish, ad enjoy!

Nutritional Value:

- Calories 130
- Total Fats 2.6g
- Carbs 0g
- Protein 24g
- Fiber: 0g

The Easiest Pesto Shrimp

Preparation Time: 20 minutes

Cooking Time: 5 minutes

Servings: 2

Ingredients:

- 1-pound Shrimp, tails and shells discarded
- ½ cup Pesto Sauce

Method:

1. Place the cleaned shrimp in a bowl and add the pesto sauce to it.
2. Mix gently with your hands, until each shrimp is coated with the sauce. Let sit for about 15 minutes.
3. In the meantime, preheat your grill to 350 degrees F.
4. Open the grill and arrange the shrimp onto the bottom plate.
5. Cook with the lid off for about 2-3 minutes. Flip over and cook for an additional 2 minutes.
6. Serve as desired and enjoy!

Nutritional Value:

- Calories 470
- Total Fats 28.5g
- Carbs 3g
- Protein 50g
- Fiber: 0g

Orange-Glazed Salmon

Preparation Time: 10 minutes
Cooking Time: 8 minutes
Servings: 4

Ingredients:

- 4 Salmon Fillets
- ½ tsp Garlic Powder
- 1 tsp Paprika
- ¼ tsp Cayenne Pepper
- 1 ¾ tsp Salt
- 1 tbsp Brown Sugar
- ¼ tsp Black Pepper

Glaze:

- 1 tsp Salt
- 2 tbsp Soy Sauce
- Juice of 1 Orange
- 4 tbsp Maple Syrup

Method:

1. Preheat your grill to medium and coat with cooking spray.
2. In a small bowl, combine the spices together, and then massage the mixture into the fish.
3. Arrange the salmon onto the bottom plate and cook with the lid off.
4. In the meantime, place the glaze ingredients in a saucepan over medium heat.
5. Cook for a couple of minutes, until thickened.
6. Once the salmon has been cooking for 3 minutes, flip it over.
7. Cook for another 3 minutes.
8. Then, brush with the glaze, lower the lid, and cook for an additional minute.
9. Serve with preferred side dish. Enjoy!

Nutritional Value:

- Calories 250
- Total Fats 19g
- Carbs 7g
- Protein 22g
- Fiber: 0g

Grilled Scallops

Preparation Time: 10 minutes
Cooking Time: 6 minutes
Servings: 4

Ingredients:

- 1-pound Jumbo Scallops
- 1 ½ tbsp Olive Oil
- ½ tsp Garlic Powder
- Salt and Pepper, to taste

Dressing:

- 1 tbsp chopped Parsley
- 3 tbsp Lemon Juice
- ½ tsp Lemon Zest
- 2 tbsp Olive Oil
- Salt and Pepper, to taste

Method:

1. Preheat your grill to medium-high.
2. Brush the scallops with olive oi, and sprinkle with salt, pepper, and garlic powder.
3. Arrange onto the bottom plate and cook for about 3 minutes, with the lid off.
4. Flip over, and grill for an additional two or three minutes.
5. Meanwhile, make the dressing by combining all of the ingredients in a small bowl.
6. Transfer the grilled scallops to a serving plate and drizzle the dressing over.
7. Enjoy!

Nutritional Value:

- Calories 102
- Total Fats 5g
- Carbs 3g
- Protein 9.5g
- Fiber: 1g

Lemon Pepper Salmon with Cherry Tomatoes and Asparagus

Preparation Time: 8 minutes

Cooking Time: 5 minutes

Servings: 4

Ingredients:

- 4 Salmon Fillets
- 8 Cherry Tomatoes
- 12 Asparagus Spears
- 2 tbsp Olive Oil
- ½ tsp Garlic Powder
- 1 tsp Lemon Pepper
- ½ tsp Onion Powder
- Salt, to taste

Method:

1. Preheat your grill to 375 degrees F and cut the tomatoes in half.
2. Brush the salmon, tomatoes, and sparagus with olive oil, and then sprinkle with the spices.
3. Arrange the salmon fillets, cherry tomatoes, and asparagus spears, onto the bottom plate.
4. Gently, lower the lid, and cook the fish and veggies for about 5-6 minutes, or until you reach your desired doneness (check at the 5th minute).
5. Serve and enjoy!

Nutritional Value:

- Calories 240
- Total Fats 14g
- Carbs 3.5g
- Protein 24g
- Fiber: 1.4g

Tuna Steak with Avocado & Mango Salsa

Preparation Time: 10 minutes
Cooking Time: 8 minutes
Servings: 2

Ingredients:

- 2 Tuna Steaks
- 1 ½ tbsp Olive Oil
- 1 tsp Paprika
- 2 tbsp Coconut Sugar
- 1 tsp Onion Powder
- ¼ tsp Pepper
- ½ tsp Salt
- 2/3 tsp Cumin

Salsa:

- 1 Avocado, pitted and diced
- 1 Mango, diced
- 1 tbsp Olive Oil
- 1 tsp Honey
- ½ Red Onion, diced
- 2 tbsp Lime Juice
- Pinch of Salt

Method:

1. Preheat your grill to 350-375 degrees F.
2. Place the olive oil and spices in a small bowl and rub the tuna steaks with the mixture.
3. Place on top of the bottom plate and cook for 4 minutes.
4. Flip the steaks over and cook for another 4 minutes.

5. Meanwhile, prepare the salsa by placing all of the salsa ingredients in a bowl, and mixing well to combine.
6. Transfer the grilled tuna steaks to two serving plates and divide the avocado and mango salsa among them.
7. Enjoy!

Nutritional Value:

- Calories 280
- Total Fats 26g
- Carbs 12g
- Protein 24g
- Fiber: 2g

Blackened Tilapia

Preparation Time: 10 minutes
Cooking Time: 8 minutes
Servings: 4

Ingredients:

- 4 Tilapia Fillets
- 3 tsp Paprika
- ½ tsp Garlic Powder
- ¼ tsp Onion Powder
- ¼ tsp Black Pepper
- ¾ tsp Salt
- 2 tbsp Olive Oil

Method:

1. Preheat your grill to 375 degrees F.
2. Place the oil and spices in a small bowl and mix to combine.
3. Rub the mixture into the tilapia fillets, making sure to coat well.
4. When the green light indicates the unit is ready for grilling, arrange the tilapia onto the bottom plate.
5. With the lid off, cook for 4 minutes.
6. Flip over, and thencook for another four minutes. Feel free to increase the cooking time if you like your fish especially burnt.
7. Serve as desired and enjoy!

Nutritional Value:

- Calories 175
- Total Fats 9g
- Carbs 1g
- Protein 23.5g
- Fiber: 0.6g

Chapter 6: Vegetarian Recipes

Goat Cheese & Tomato Stuffed Zucchini

Preparation Time: 2 minutes
Cooking Time: 8 minutes
Servings: 8

Ingredients:

- 14 ounces Goat Cheese
- 1 ½ cups Tomato Sauce
- 4 medium Zucchini

Method:

1. Preheat your grill to medium-high.
2. Cut the zucchini in half and scoop the seeds out.
3. Coat the grill with cooking spray and add the zucchini to it.
4. Lower the lid and cook for 2 minutes.
5. Now, add half of the goat cheese first, top with tomato sauce, and place the remaining cheese on top. Place a piece of aluminum foil on top of the filling so you don't make a big mess.
6. Carefully lower the grill and cook for an additional minute.
7. Serve and enjoy!

Nutritional Value:

- Calories 170
- Total Fats 11g
- Carbs 8.2g
- Protein 10.5g
- Fiber: 2.3g

Haloumi Kebobs

Preparation Time: 15 minutes
Cooking Time: 5 minutes
Servings: 4

Ingredients:

- ½ pound Haloumi Cheese
- 4 Cremini Mushrooms, cut in half
- 1 Zucchini, cut into chunks
- ½ Bell Pepper, cut into chunks
- 2 tbsp Olive Oil
- Salt and Pepper, to taste

Method:

1. Preheat your grill to 375 degrees F.
2. Meanwhile, soak 8 wooden skewers in water to preven burning.
3. Cut the cheese int chunks.
4. Thread the cheese and veggies onto the skewers, drizzle with the olive oil and sprinkle with salt and pepper.
5. Arrange onto the bottom plate, lower the lid, and cook closed for about 5 minutes (or more if you want it well-done).
6. Serve as desired and enjoy!

Nutritional Value:

- Calories 220
- Total Fats 14g
- Carbs 6g
- Protein 5g
- Fiber: 1.2g

Paprika & Chipotle Lime Cauli-steaks

Preparation Time: 10 minutes
Cooking Time: 6 minutes
Servings: 4

Ingredients:

- 2 Cauliflower Heads
- 4 tbsp Olive Oil
- 1 tsp minced Garlic
- 1 tbsp Chipotle Powder
- 1 ½ tbsp Paprika
- 1 tsp Honey
- 1 tsp Salt
- Juice of 1 large Lime
- 1 tsp Lime Zest

Method:

1. Preheat your grill to medium-high.
2. Remove the outter leaves of the cauliflower and trim them well. Lay them flat onto your cutting board and then cut into steak-like pieces. (about 3 to 4 inches thick).
3. In a bowl, whisk together all of the remaining ingredients.
4. Brush the steaks with the mixture well, and then arrange them onto the bottom plate of the grill.
5. Lower the lid to cut the cooking time in half, and cook only for about 6 minutes, without turning over.
6. Transfer to a serving plate and enjoy!

Nutritional Value:

- Calories 202
- Total Fats 14g
- Carbs 16g
- Protein 6g
- Fiber: 8g

Grilled Pizza Margarita

Preparation Time: 8 minutes
Cooking Time: 2 minutes
Servings: 1

Ingredients:

- 1 Tortilla
- 3 tbsp Tomato Sauce
- 3 ounces shredded Mozzarella
- 4 Basil Leaves, chopped
- Pinch of Salt

Method:

1. Preheat your grill to medium-high.
2. Unlock to lower the griddle and lay it on your counter.
3. When the green light turns on, add the tortilla to the grill, and lower the lid.
4. Cook only for about 40 seconds, just until it becomes hot.
5. Add the tomato sauce on top, sprinkle with cheese, basil, and some salt.
6. Cook for another minute or so – with the lid OFF – until the cheese becomes melted.
7. Serve and enjoy!

Nutritional Value:

- Calories 375
- Total Fats 22g
- Carbs 23g
- Protein 22g
- Fiber: 2g

Grilled Tofu with Pineapple

Preparation Time: 15 minutes
Cooking Time: 8 minutes
Servings: 4

Ingredients:

- 1 pound firm Tofu
- 1 Red Bell Pepper
- 1 Yello Bell Pepper
- 1 Zucchini
- ½ Pineapple
- ½ tsp Ginger Paste
- Salt and Pepper, to taste
- 2 tbsp Olive Oil

Method:

1. Preheat your grill to medium-high.
2. Meanwhile, chop the tofu and vegies into smaller chunks, and place in a bowl. If using wooden skewers, soak them into water before using.
3. Add ginger and oil to the bowl and mix until coated well.
4. Thread the veggies and tofu onto the skewers.
5. When the green light turns on, open the grill and arrange the skewers onto the bottom plate.
6. Cook for 4 minutes, then flip over and cook for additional four minutes.
7. Serve as desired and enjoy!

Nutritional Value:

- Calories 210
- Total Fats 12g
- Carbs 9g
- Protein 12g
- Fiber: 2g

Caprese Eggplant Boats

Preparation Time: 10 minutes
Cooking Time: 10 minutes
Servings: 4

Ingredients:

- 2 Eggplants
- 1 cup Cherry Tomatoes, halved
- 1 cup Mozzarella Balls, chopped
- 2 tbsp Olive Oil
- 4 tbsp chopped Basil Leaves
- Salt and Pepper, to taste

Method:

1. Preheat your grill to 375 degrees F.
2. Cut the eggplants in half (no need to peel them- just wash well), drizzle with olive oil and season with salt and pepper, generously.
3. When the green light is on, open the grill and arrange the eggplant halves onto the bottom plate.
4. Lower the lid and cook for about 4-5 minutes, until well-done.
5. Transfer to a serving plate and top with cherry tomatoes, mozzarella and basil.
6. Serve and enjoy!

Nutritional Value:

- Calories 187
- Total Fats 11g
- Carbs 18.3g
- Protein 6.8g
- Fiber: 7.3g

Spinach and Cheese Portobellos

Preparation Time: 10 minutes
Cooking Time: 6 minutes
Servings: 3

Ingredients:

- 3 Portobello Mushrooms
- 2 cups Spinach, chopped
- 1 cup shredded Cheddar Cheese
- 4 ounces Cream Cheese
- 1 tbsp Olive Oil
- 1 tsp minced Garlic
- Salt and Pepper, to taste

Method:

1. Preheat your grill to 350 degrees F.
2. Clean the mushroom caps well, and pat dry with paper towels.
3. Remove the stems, so the fillign can fit.
4. Now, make the filling by mixing the cheeses, spinach, and garlic. Divide this mixture among the mushrooms.
5. Drizzle with olive oil.
6. When the green light is on, open the grill and add the mushrooms.
7. Arrange on top of the plate and cook with the lid off for about 5 minutes.
8. Now, lower the lid gently, but do not use pressure. Let cook for 15-20 seconds, just so the cheese melts faster.
9. Transfer to a serving plate and enjoy!

Nutritional Value:

- Calories 210
- Total Fats 9g
- Carbs 5g
- Protein 10g
- Fiber: 1g

Chapter 7: Salad Recipes

Pork and Veggie Salad

Preparation Time: 2 minutes
Cooking Time: 8 minutes
Servings: 1

Ingredients:

- ½ pound Pork Tenderloin
- 1 Lettuce Head
- 1 Tomato, chopped
- 1 Cucumber, chopped
- 1 can Beans, drained
- 1 Carrot, julienned
- 2 tbsp Olive Oil
- 2 tbsp Sour Cream
- 1 tsp Dijon Mustard
- 1 tsp Lemon Juice
- 1 tbsp Honey
- Salt and Pepper, to taste

Method:

1. Preheat your grill to medium-high.
2. Cut the pork into strips and season with salt and pepper.
3. Coat the grill with cooking spray and arrange the pork onto the bottom plate.
4. Lower the lid so you can cut the cooking time in half and cook for 5 minutes.
5. When done, transfer to a cutting board.
6. If you want to, you can cut the pork into even smaller bite-sized pieces at this point.
7. Add the oil, lemon juice, mustard, honey, sour cream, and some salt and pepper, to a large bowl.
8. Mix well to combine and add the veggies.

9. Toss well to coat.
10. Top the salad with the grilled pork.
11. Enjoy!

Nutritional Value:

- Calories 240
- Total Fats 18g
- Carbs 15g
- Protein 20g
- Fiber: 2g

Grilled Zucchini and Feta Salad

Preparation Time: 10 minutes
Cooking Time: 3 minutes
Servings: 4

Ingredients:

- 1 Large Zucchini
- 1 cup Baby Spinach
- ½ cup crumbled Feta Cheese
- 1 cup Cherry Tomatoes, cut in half
- 1 cup Corn
- 3 tbsp Olive Oil
- 1 tsp Lemon Juice
- Salt and Pepper, to taste

Method:

1. Preheat your grill to 350 degrees F.
2. Peel the zucchini and slice lengthwise. Season with salt and pepper.
3. Open the grill and coat with cooking spray.
4. Arrange the zucchini on top of the bottom plate and lower the lid.
5. Cook for 2-3 minutes.
6. Meanwhile, combine the remaining ingredients in a large bowl.
7. Transfer the zucchini to cutting bord and chop into pieces.
8. Add to the bowl and toss well to combine.
9. Serve and enjoy!

Nutritional Value:

- Calories 192
- Total Fats 14.6g
- Carbs 12.6g
- Protein 5g
- Fiber: 2.7g

Rib Eye Steak Salad

Preparation Time: 10 minutes
Cooking Time: 5 minutes
Servings: 4

Ingredients:

- 1 ½ pounds Rib Eye Steaks
- ¼ cup Fish Sauce
- ½ cup Mint Leaves
- 4 tbsp Lime Juice
- ½ cup Coriander Leaves
- 1 Lettuce Head
- 1 cup halved Cherry Tomatoes
- Salt and Pepper, to taste

Method:

1. Preheat your grill to 375 degrees F. Spray with cooking spray.
2. Season the steak with salt and pepper and cut into strips.
3. When ready, arrange the steak onto the bottom plate.
4. Lower the lid and cook for 4-5 minutes, depending on the doneness you wish to achieve. Transfer to a plate.
5. Chop the lettuce and add to a bowl.
6. Add the rest of the ingredients and toss well to combine and coat.
7. Top the salad with the grilled steak.
8. Serve and enjoy!

Nutritional Value:

- Calories 350
- Total Fats 30g
- Carbs 10g
- Protein 31g
- Fiber: 1g

Grilled Watermelon Salad with Cucumber and Cheese

Preparation Time: 10 minutes

Cooking Time: 4 minutes

Servings: 4

Ingredients:

- 1 Small Watermelon (approximately yielding 4 cups when cubed)
- 1 tbsp chopped Basil
- 1 Cucumber, chopped
- 3 ounces Feta Cheese, crumbled or cubed
- Juice of 1 Lime
- 1 tbsp Olive Oil
- Salt and Pepper, to taste

Method:

1. Preheat your grill to medium.
2. Peel and slice the watermelon (discard any seeds).
3. Open the grill and arrange the watermelon onto the bottom plate.
4. Lower the lid and cook for 4 minutes.
5. Transfer to a cutting board and slice into chunks.
6. Place into a bowl and add the rest of the ingredients.
7. Toss well to combine and coat.
8. Serve and enjoy!

Nutritional Value:

- Calories 122
- Total Fats 5g
- Carbs 17g
- Protein 4g
- Fiber: 1g

Chicken Caesar Salad

Preparation Time: 10 minutes
Cooking Time: 6 minutes
Servings: 4

Ingredients:

- 4 Chicken Breasts, boneless and skinless
- 1 Lettuce Head
- 1/3 cup Olive Oil
- ½ tsp Dijon Mustard
- 1 tsp Lemon Juice
- ½ cup grated Parmesan Cheese
- ½ tsp Anchovy Paste
- 1 tsp Red Wine Vinegar
- 1 tsp Worcestershire Sauce
- 1 cup Croutons
- 1 tsp Honey
- Salt and Pepper, to taste

Method:

1. Preheat your grill to medium-high heat.
2. When the green light turns on, open the grill and coat with cooking spray.
3. Season the chicken with salt and pepper and place onto the bottom plate.
4. Lower the lid and cook the chicken for 6 full minutes.
5. Transfer to a cutting board and cut into strips.
6. Chop the lettuce head and place in a bowl. Add the chicken and croutons to the bowl.
7. In a smaller bowl, whisk together the remaining ingredients and drizzle the salad with the mixture.
8. Serve and enjoy!

Nutritional Value:

- Calories 540
- Total Fats 35g
- Carbs 15g
- Protein 45g
- Fiber: 4g

Shrimp Salad with Sour Cream and Dijon

Preparation Time: 10 minutes

Cooking Time: 6 minutes

Servings: 4

Ingredients:

- 1-pound Shrimp
- 1 Lettuce Head
- 1 cup Baby Spinach
- 1 Cucumber
- 1 Tomato
- 1 tbsp chopped Parsley
- ½ cup Sour Cream
- 2 tbsp Lemon Juice
- 1 tbsp Honey
- 1 tbsp Dijon Mustard
- 2 tbsp Olive Oil
- Salt and Pepper, to taste

Method:

1. Preheat your grill to medium-high.
2. When the green light is on, grease with cooking spray.
3. Season the shrimp with salt and pepper and arrange onto the bottom plate.
4. Cook for 2-3 minutes, then flip over, and cook for 2-3 minutes more.
5. Meanwhile, chop the veggies and place in a large bowl.
6. When ready, transfer the shrimp to the bowl.
7. In another bowl, whisk together the remaining ingredients.
8. Drizzle the sour cream mixture over the salad.
9. Serve and enjoy!

Nutritional Value:

- Calories 245
- Total Fats 16g
- Carbs 12g
- Protein 20g
- Fiber: 2.2g

Greek Grilled Salmon Salad

Preparation Time: 10 minutes
Cooking Time: 8 minutes
Servings: 4

Ingredients:

- 1-pound Salmon Fillets
- 4 cups chopped Lettuce
- 1 Red Onion, sliced
- 1/3 cup Kalamata Olives, pitted
- 1 Cucumber, chopped
- 1 Avocado, sliced
- 2 Tomatoes, chopped
- ½ cup Feta Cheese, crumbled
- 3 tbsp Olive Oil
- 1 tsp Oregano
- 1 tsp Basil
- 2 tbsp Lemon Juice
- Salt and Pepper, to taste

Method:

1. Preheat your grill to medium-high.
2. When ready, open the grill and coat with cooking spray.
3. Season the salmon with salt and pepper and arrange onto the bottom plate.
4. Grill open, for about 4 minutes. Flip over, and grill for another 3 to 4 minutes.
5. Transfer to a cutting board and slice.
6. Place the veggies in a large bowl and toss to combine well.
7. Top the salad with the grilled salmon slices and feta cheese.
8. In a smaller bowl, whisk together the olive oil, lemon juice, oregano, basil, and some salt and pepper. Drizzel over the salad.
9. Serve and enjoy!

Nutritional Value:

- Calories 411
- Total Fats 27g
- Carbs 12g
- Protein 28g
- Fiber: 6g

Chapter 8: Sandwich Recipes

Fish Tacos with Slaw and Mango Salsa

Preparation Time: 10 minutes
Cooking Time: 6 minutes
Servings: 4

Ingredients:

- 4 Tortillas
- 1-pound Cod
- 3 tbsp butter, melted
- ½ tsp Paprika
- ¼ tsp Garlic Onion
- 1 tsp Thyme
- ½ tsp Onion Powder
- ½ tsp Cayenne Pepper
- 1 tsp Brown Sugar
- 1 cup prepared (or store-brought) Slaw
- Salt and Pepper, to taste

Mango Salsa:

- ¼ cup diced Red Onions
- Juice of 1 Lime
- 1 Mango, diced
- 1 Jalapeno Pepper, deseeded and minced
- 1 tbsp chopped Parlsey or Cilantro

Method:

1. Preheat your grill to medium.
2. Brush the butter over the cod and sprinkle with the spices.
3. When ready, open the grill, and arrange the cod fillets onto the bottom plate.

4. Lower the lid and cook for about 4-5 minutes in total.
5. Transfer to a plate and cut into chunks.
6. Place all of the mango salsa ingredients in a bowl and mix to combine.
7. Assemble the tacos by adding slaw, topping with grilled cod, and adding a tablespoon or so of the mango salsa.
8. Enjoy!

Nutritional Value:

- Calories 323
- Total Fats 12g
- Carbs 31g
- Protein 24g
- Fiber: 3g

Chicken Pesto Grilled Sandwich

Preparation Time: 10 minutes
Cooking Time: 4 minutes
Servings: 2

Ingredients:

- 4 Slices of Bread
- 1 ½ cups shredded Mozzarella Cheese
- ½ cup Pesto Sauce
- 2 cups cooked and shredded Chicken Meat
- 8 Sundried Tomatoes
- 1 ½ tbsp Butter

Method:

1. Preheat your grill to medium-high.
2. Combine the pesto and chicken in a bowl.
3. Brush the outsides of the bread with the butter.
4. Divide the pesto/chicken filling between two bread slices.
5. Top with sundried tomatoes and mozzarella cheese.
6. Open the grill and carefully transfer the loaded slices of bread onto the top bottom.
7. Top with the remaining bread slices, carefully.
8. Lower the lid, pressing gently.
9. Let the sandwiches cook for about 3-4 minutes, or until the desired doneness is reached.
10. Serve and enjoy!

Nutritional Value:

- Calories 725
- Total Fats 44.5g
- Carbs 32g
- Protein 51g
- Fiber: 7.5g

The Greatest Butter Burger Recipe

Preparation Time: 10 minutes
Cooking Time: 11 minutes
Servings: 6

Ingredients:

- 2 pounds Ground Chuck Meat
- 1 ½ tsp minced Garlic
- 6 tbsp Butter
- 2 tbsp Worcestershire Sauce
- 1 tsp Salt
- ½ tsp Pepper
- 6 Hamburger Buns
- Veggie Toppings of Choice

Method:

1. Preheat your grill to medium-high.
2. Meanwhile, place the meat, garlic, sauce, salt, and pepper, in a bowl.
3. Mix with your hands to incorporate well. Make six patties out of the mixture.
4. Into each patty, press about one tablespoon into the center.
5. Open the grill and coat with some cooking spray.
6. Arrange the patties onto the bottom plate and cook for 6 minutes.
7. Flip over and cook for 5 more minutes.
8. Serve in hamburger buns with desired veggie toppings.
9. Enjoy!

Nutritional Value:

- Calories 595
- Total Fats 48g
- Carbs 25g
- Protein 27g
- Fiber: 1.5g

Cheesy Buffalo Avocado Sandwich

Preparation Time: 15 minutes
Cooking Time: 4 minutes
Servings: 4

Ingredients:

- 1 Avocado
- 2 Bread Slices
- 2 slices Cheddar Cheese
- 1 tbsp Butter

Buffalo Sauce:

- 4 tbsp Hot Sauce
- 1 tbs White Vinegar
- ¼ cup Butter
- ¼ tsp Salt
- 1 tsp Cayenne Pepper
- ¼ tsp Garlic Salt

Method:

1. Preheat your grill to 375 degrees F.
2. Meanwhile, peel the avocado, scoop out the flash, and mash it with a fork.
3. Spread the avocado onto a bread slice, and top with the cheddar cheese.
4. Spread the butter onto the outside of the other bread slice.
5. Top the sandwich with the buttery slice, with the butter-side up.
6. Grease the bottom cooking plate and place the sandwich there, with the butter-side up.
7. Lower the lid, press, and let the sandwich grill for about 4 minutes.
8. Meanwhile, whisk together all of the sauce ingredients.
9. Serve the sandwich with the Buffalo sauce and enjoy!

Nutritional Value:

- Calories 485
- Total Fats 24g
- Carbs 35g
- Protein 8g
- Fiber: 3g

Simple Pork Chop Sandwich

Preparation Time: 10 minutes

Cooking Time: 7 minutes

Servings: 4

Ingredients:

- 4 Hamburger Buns
- 4 Cheddar Slices
- 4 boneless Pork Chop
- Salt and Pepper, to taste
- 4 tbsp Mayonnaise

Method:

1. Preheat your grill to 375 degrees F.
2. When the green light turns on, open the grill.
3. Season the pork chops with salt and pepper and arrange onto the bottom plate.
4. Lower the lid, and cook the meat closed, for about 5-6 minutes.
5. Open the lid and place a slice of cheddar on top of each chop.
6. Cook for another minute or so, uncovered, until the cheese starts to melt.
7. Spread a tbsp of mayonnaise onto the insides of each bun.
8. Place the cheesy pork chop inside and serve.
9. Enjoy!

Nutritional Value:

- Calories 510
- Total Fats 30.6g
- Carbs 18.4g
- Protein 42g
- Fiber: 5g

Buttery Pepperoni Grilled Cheese Sandwich

Preparation Time: 10 minutes

Cooking Time: 5 minutes

Servings: 2

Ingredients:

- 4 slices of Bread
- 4 slices of Mozzarella Cheese
- 4 tbsp Butter
- 18 Pepperoni Slices

Method:

1. Preheat your grill to medium-high.
2. Meanwhile, brush each slice of bread with a tablespoon of butter. It seems like too much, but the taste is just incredible.
3. Divide the mozzarella and pepperoni among the insides of two bread slices.
4. Top the sandwich with the other slices of bread, keeping the buttery side up.
5. When the green light appears, open the grill.
6. Place the sandwiches carefully onto the bottom plate.
7. Lower the lid, and gently press.
8. Allow the sandwich to cook for 4-5 minutes.
9. Open the lid, transfer to a serving plate, cut in half, and serve. Enjoy!

Nutritional Value:

- Calories 625
- Total Fats 46g
- Carbs 29g
- Protein 22g
- Fiber: 2g

Chicken Burgers

Preparation Time: 10 minutes
Cooking Time: 8 minutes
Servings: 4

Ingredients:

- 4 Hamburger Buns
- 8 Red Onion Rings
- 4 slices of Provolone Cheese
- 4 Lettuce Leaves
- 1 Avocado, scooped out and mashed
- 4 Chicken Breast Halves, boneless and skinless
- 1 tbsp Olive Oil
- 1 tsp Garlic Powder
- ½ tsp Paprika
- ¼ tsp Cumin
- ¼ tsp Oregano
- ¼ tsp Basil
- ¼ tsp Turmeric Powder
- Salt and Pepper, to taste

Method:

1. Preheat your grill to medium high.
2. Combine the oil and spices together, and gently rub the meat with this mixture.
3. Open the grill when the green light turns on and place the chicken on top of the bottom grill.
4. Cook for about 4 minutes, then flip over, and cook for another four minutes on the other side.
5. Meanwhile, cut the buns in half and divide the avocado between four halves. Add the lettuce leave on top.
6. Place the chicken on top of the lettuce and top with the cheese and onion rings.

7. Top the sandwich with the remaining bun halves.
8. Serve and enjoy!

Nutritional Value:

- Calories 480
- Total Fats 23g
- Carbs 31g
- Protein 37g
- Fiber: 6g

Chapter 9: Side Dishes Recipes

Brussel Sprout Skewers

Preparation Time: 10 minutes
Cooking Time: 7 minutes
Servings: 8

Ingredients:

- 24 Brussel Sprouts
- 2 tbsp Balsamic Glaze
- 4 tbsp Olive Oil
- ½ tsp Garlic Powder
- Salt and Pepper, to taste

Method:

1. Preheat your grill to 375 degrees F.
2. In the meantime, trim the brussel sprouts and cut the in half.
3. Thread onto soaked wooden or metal skewers.
4. Drizzle with olive oil and sprinkle with the seasonings.
5. Place onto the bottom plate and cook uncovered for 4 minutes.
6. Turn over and cook for another 3 minutes or so.
7. Serve as desired and enjoy!

Nutritional Value:

- Calories 92
- Total Fats 6g
- Carbs 6g
- Protein 1g
- Fiber: 2g

Grilled Zucchini

Preparation Time: 65 minutes
Cooking Time: 6 minutes
Servings: 4

Ingredients:

- 1-pound Zucchini
- 1 tbsp Lemon Juice
- 2 Garlic Cloves, minced
- 2 tbsp Olive Oil
- 1 tsp Italian Seasoning
- Salt and Pepper, to taste

Method:

1. Trim and peel the zucchini. Cut into thick slices and place in a bowl.
2. Add all of the remaining ingredients and mix well so that the zucchini slices are completely coated.
3. Cover the bowl and place in the fridge for about one hour.
4. Menawhile, preheat your HB grill to 375 degrees F.
5. When the green light turns on, open the grill and place the zucchini slices onto the bottom plate.
6. Cook with the lid off, for three minutes. Flip over and cook for another three minutes.
7. Serve as desired and enjoy!

Nutritional Value:

- Calories 76
- Total Fats 7g
- Carbs 1g
- Protein 0g
- Fiber: 0g

Balsamic-Glazed Carrots

Preparation Time: 10 minutes

Cooking Time: 6 minutes

Servings: 10

Ingredients:

- 2 pounds Carrots, boiled for 3-4 minutes
- 3 tbsp Balsamic Vinegar
- 1 tsp ground Ginger
- 1 tsp Thyme
- 1 ½ tbsp Maple Syrup
- ½ tbsp Lime Juice
- Salt and Pepper, to taste

Method:

1. Preheat your grill to 400 degrees F.
2. Meanwhile, cut the carrots in half lengthwise.
3. Place the remaining ingredients in a bowl and whisk well to combine.
4. Brush the carrots with the mixture, on all sides.
5. When the green light is on, open the grill and spray with some cooking spray.
6. Arrange the carrots on top of the bottom plate and cook for 3 minutes.
7. Flip over and cook for 3 more minutes on the other side.
8. Serve and enjoy!

Nutritional Value:

- Calories 50
- Total Fats 1g
- Carbs 12g
- Protein 1g
- Fiber: 3g

Italian-Seasoned Grilled Veggies

Preparation Time: 15 minutes
Cooking Time: 8 minutes
Servings: 8

Ingredients:

- 1 Zucchini, cut into chunks
- 1 Squash, cut into chunks
- 8 ounces Button Mushrooms, quartered
- 1 Red Bell Pepper, chopped
- 1 Red Onion, cut into chunks
- 2 tbsp Balsamic Vinegar
- 4 tbsp Olive Oil
- 2 tbsp Italian Seasoning
- 4 tbsp grated Parmesan Cheese
- Juice of 1 Lemon
- ½ tsp Garlic Powder

Method:

1. Preheat your grill to medium-high heat.
2. In a bowl, place all of the ingredient, except the Parmesan Cheese.
3. With your hands, mix well so that each chunk of veggie is coated with oil and seasoning.
4. Thread the veggie chunks onto metal skewers (You can also use soaked wooden ones).
5. When the grill is ready, open the lid, and arrange the skewers onto the bottom plate.
6. Without covering the lid, cook for about 4 minutes.
7. Flip the skewers over and cook for another 3-4 minutes.
8. Serve sprinkled with Parmesan cheese and enjoy!

Nutritional Value:

- Calories 110
- Total Fats 8g
- Carbs 7.5g
- Protein 3g
- Fiber: 2.5g

Grilled and Dressed Romaine Head

Preparation Time: 5 minutes
Cooking Time: 5 minutes
Servings: 4

Ingredients

- 2 Hearts of Romaine
- ½ cup Olive Oil
- 2 Eg Yolks
- 2 Whole Garlic Cloves
- ½ tsp Dijon Mustard
- 2 Anchovies
- 3 tbsp Parmesan Cheese
- 4 tbsp Lemon Juice
- Salt an Pepper, to taste

Method:

1. Preheat your grill to medium high.
2. Place all of the dressing ingredients to the bowl of your food processor.
3. Pulse until smooth and set aside.
4. When the grill is ready, open the lid and spray with some cooking spray.
5. Place the romaine heart onto the bottom plate and cook for 3 minutes.
6. Flip over and cook for 2 more minutes.
7. Arrange on a large serving plate.
8. Drizzle with the dressing.
9. Enjoy!

Nutritional Value:

- Calories 88
- Total Fats 4g
- Carbs 3g
- Protein 2.5g
- Fiber: 0.4g

Garlicky Mushroom Skewers with Balsamic Vinegar

Preparation Time: 40 minutes
Cooking Time: 4 minutes
Servings: 4

Ingredients:

- 2 pounds Button Mushrooms, halved
- 1 tbsp Tamari Sauce
- 2 tbsp Balsamic Vinegar
- ½ tsp Dried Thyme
- 2 large Garlic Cloves, minced
- Salt and Pepper, to taste

Method:

1. Place the tamari, balsamic, thyme, and garlic, in a bowl.
2. Season with some salt and pepper and mix well to combine.
3. Add the mushrooms and toss to coat them well.
4. Cover the bowl and place in the fridge for about 30 minutes.
5. While the mushrooms are marinating, soak your wooden skewers in water to prevent burning.
6. Preheat your grill to 375 degrees F.
7. Thread the mushrooms onto your skewers and place on top of the bottom plate.
8. Grill for 2 minutes, then flip over, and grill for another two minutes, or until tender.
9. Serve and enjoy!

Nutritional Value:

- Calories 62
- Total Fats 1g
- Carbs 9g
- Protein 7g
- Fiber: 2g

Mayo & Parmesan Corn on the Cob

Preparation Time: 5 minutes
Cooking Time: 15 minutes
Servings: 4

Ingredients:

- 4 Ears of Corn
- 1 cup grated Parmesan Cheese
- ½ cup Mayonnaise
- Juice of 1 Lemon
- 1 cup Sour Cream
- ½ tsp Cayenne Pepper
- 4 tbsp chopped Cilantro

Method:

1. Preheat your grill to medium-high heat.
2. Clean the corn by removing the husk and silk.
3. When the grill is ready, open the lid and place the corn on top of the bottom plate.
4. Cook for about 10 to 15 minutes, rotating occasionally while grilling.
5. Meanwhile, combine the sour cream, mayonnaise, and cilantro.
6. Brush the grilled corn with this mixture, and generously sprinkle with Parmesan cheese.
7. Drizzle the lime juice over before serving. Enjoy!

Nutritional Value:

- Calories 428
- Total Fats 34g
- Carbs 22g
- Protein 11g
- Fiber: 2g

Chapter 10: Snack Recipes

Grilled Pineapple with Coconut Sauce

Preparation Time: 10 minutes

Cooking Time: 8 minutes

Servings: 4

Ingredients:

- 1 large Pineapple
- 1 ½ tsp Cornstarch
- 2 tbsp Coconut Rum
- 1 tbsp Butter
- 1 tbsp Cream of Coconut

Method:

1. Preheat your grill to medium high.
2. In the meantime, prepare the pineapple. Peel and slice into the size of your preference.
3. Thread the pineapple slices onto soaked skewers and open the grill.
4. Arrange on top of the bottom plate and grill for about 4 minutes per side.
5. In the meantime, whisk together the remaining ingredients in a saucepan.
6. Place over medium heat and cook until slightly thickened.
7. Serve the pineapple alongside the sauce.
8. Enjoy!

Nutritional Value:

- Calories 235
- Total Fats 10g
- Carbs 34g
- Protein 2g
- Fiber: 3g

Veggie Sliders

Preparation Time: 10 minutes
Cooking Time: 7 minutes
Servings: 10

Ingredients:

- ½ Red Onion, diced
- ¾ cup cooked Quinoa
- 15 ounces canned Kidney
- ½ cup Walnuts, crushed or ground
- 1 shake Worcestershire Sauce
- 1 tbsp Chili Powder
- Salt and Pepper, to taste

Method:

1. Preheat your grill to 350-375 degrees F.
2. Dump all of the ingredients in a bowl and mix well with your hands to incorporate the mixture.
3. Make about 10 small patties with your hands.
4. When ready, open the grill and coat with cooking spray.
5. Arrange the patties on top of the bottom plate.
6. Lower the lid and cook closed for about 6-7 minutes.
7. Serve on top of a lettuce leaf. Enjoy!

Nutritional Value:

- Calories 89
- Total Fats 4.2g
- Carbs 9g
- Protein 4g
- Fiber: 3g

Grilled Melon with Honey & Lime

Preparation Time: 10 minutes
Cooking Time: 6 minutes
Servings: 4

Ingredients:

- ½ small Melon
- 2 tbsp Honey
- Juice of 1 Lime
- Pinch of Salt
- Pinch of Pepper

Method:

1. Preheat your grill to medium high.
2. In the meantime, peel the melon and cut into wedges.
3. When the green light appears, open the grill and coat with cooking spray.
4. Arrange the melon wedges onto the bottom plate of your HB grill.
5. Cook for about 3 minutes.
6. Flip over and cook for another three minutes.
7. Whisk together the honey, lime, salt, and pepper, and brush the grilled melon with this mixture.
8. Serve and enjoy!

Nutritional Value:

- Calories 92
- Total Fats 2g
- Carbs 24g
- Protein 2g
- Fiber: 4g

Bacon-Wrapped Peppers

Preparation Time: 10 minutes
Cooking Time: 6 minutes
Servings: 4

Ingredients:

- 4 ounces Cream Cheese, softened
- 8 smallish Peppers
- 4 Bacon Slices

Method:

1. Preheat your grill to 375 degrees F.
2. Cut of the top of the peppers and fiscard the seeds.
3. Fill the peppers with the cheese.
4. Cut the bacon slices in half, lengthwise, and wrap each pepper with it.
5. Open the grill and unlock the hinge.
6. Make sure the kickstand is in place.
7. Arrange the peppers onto the grill and cook for about 3 minutes.
8. Flip over and cook for another three minutes.
9. Serve and enjoy!

Nutritional Value:

- Calories 156
- Total Fats 13g
- Carbs 5g
- Protein 1.1g
- Fiber: 6.2g

Shrimp & Pineapple Kabobs

Preparation Time: 25 minutes
Cooking Time: 6 minutes
Servings: 6

Ingredients:

- 18 large Shrimp, cleaned
- 4 tbsp Honey
- 4 tbsp Soy Sauce
- 12 Pineapple Chunks
- 4 tbsp Balsamic Vinegar
- Salt and Pepper, to taste

Method:

1. Thread the shrimp and pineapple onto skewers (no need to soak them) and place in a Ziploc bag.
2. In a bowl, whisk together the remaining ingredients.
3. Pour the mixture over the shrimp and pinapple.
4. Seal the bag and let marinate in the fridge for 15 minutes.
5. Meanwhile, preheat your grill to medium.
6. Once ready, open the grill and arrange the skewers onto the bottom plate.
7. Grill without lowering the lid, for 3 minutes per side.
8. Serve and enjoy!

Nutritional Value:

- Calories 61
- Total Fats 1g
- Carbs 11g
- Protein 4g
- Fiber: 1g

Grilled Tomatoes with Garlic & Parmesan

Preparation Time: 10 minutes

Cooking Time: 6 minutes

Servings: 8

Ingredients:

- ½ cup grated Parmesan Cheese
- 8 small Tomatoes, halved
- 1 tsp Garlic Powder
- 2 tbsp Olive Oil
- ¼ tsp Onion Powder
- Salt and Pepper, to taste

Method:

1. Preheat your grill to 350 degrees F.
2. Combine the oil, garlic powder, onion powder, and salt and pepper, in a bowl.
3. Brush the tomatoes with this mixture.
4. Open the grill and arrange the tomatoes onto the plate.
5. Cook for 3 minutes, then flip over and cook for 2 more minutes.
6. Top with the parmesan cheese and cook for an additional minute.
7. Serve and enjoy!

Nutritional Value:

- Calories 78
- Total Fats 5.6g
- Carbs 4.5g
- Protein 3.4g
- Fiber: 1g

Zucchini Rollups with Hummus

Preparation Time: 15 minutes
Cooking Time: 3 minutes
Servings: 4

Ingredients:

- 2 medium Zucchini
- 6 tbsp Hummus
- 1 tbsp Olive Oil
- 1 Roasted Red Pepper, diced
- Salt and Pepper, to taste

Method:

1. Preheat your grill to medium high.
2. Peel and slice the zucchini lengthwise.
3. Brush with olive oil and season with salt and pepper, generously.
4. Open the grill and arrange the zucchini slices on top.
5. Close the grill and cook for 2-3 minutes.
6. Transfer to a serving plate and let cool a bit until safe to handle.
7. Divide the hummus and red pepper among the grilled zucchini.
8. Roll up and secure the filling with a toothpick.
9. Serve and enjoy!

Nutritional Value:

- Calories 43
- Total Fats 3.1g
- Carbs 3.6g
- Protein 1g
- Fiber: 1g

Chapter 11: Dessert Recipes

Grilled Watermelon & Cream

Preparation Time: 10 minutes
Cooking Time: 4 minutes
Servings: 8

Ingredients:

- 1 medium Watermelon
- 3 cups Whipped Cream
- 2 tbsp chopped Mint

Method:

1. Preheat your grill to medium high.
2. Peel the melon and cut into wedges. Discard seeds if there are any.
3. Open the grill and arrange the wedges on top of the bottom plate.
4. Lower te lid and cook for 3-4 minutes.
5. Open and transfer to a cutting board.
6. Cut into smaller chunks and let cool.
7. Divide among 8 serving glasses.
8. Top with whipped cream and mint leaves.
9. Enjoy!

Nutritional Value:

- Calories 323
- Total Fats 17.3g
- Carbs 44g
- Protein 4.4g
- Fiber: 2.2g

Cinnamon Sugar Grilled Apricots

Preparation Time: 10 minutes
Cooking Time: 6 minutes
Servings: 4

Ingredients:

- 6 smallish Apricots
- 1 tbsp Butter, melted
- 3 tbsp Brown Sugar
- ½ tbsp Cinnamon

Method:

1. Preheat your grill to 350 degrees F.
2. Cut the apricots in half and discard the seeds.
3. When ready, open the grill and coat with cooking spray.
4. Arrange the apricots and cook for 3 minutes.
5. Flip over and cook for 3 minutes more.
6. Meanwhile, whisk together the butter, sugar, and cinnamon.
7. Transfer the grilled apricots to a serving plate.
8. Drizzle the sauce over.
9. Enjoy!

Nutritional Value:

- Calories 92
- Total Fats 2g
- Carbs 17g
- Protein 1g
- Fiber: 1g

Chocolate-Covered Grilled Strawberries

Preparation Time: 10 minutes
Cooking Time: 6 minutes
Servings: 4

Ingredients:

- 12 Large Strawberries
- 3 ounces Chocolate
- 1 tbsp Butter

Method:

1. Preheat your grill to 350 degrees F.
2. Clean and hull the strawberries.
3. When the green light appears, arrange the strawberries onto the plate.
4. Grill for about 6 minutes, rotating occasionally for even cooking.
5. Melt the chocolate and butter in a microwave. Stir to combine.
6. Coat the grilled strawberries with the melted chocolate and arrange on a platter.
7. Let harden before consuming.
8. Enjoy!

Nutritional Value:

- Calories 146
- Total Fats 8g
- Carbs 18.3g
- Protein 1.4g
- Fiber: 1.6g

Fruity Skewers

Preparation Time: 10 minutes
Cooking Time: 6 minutes
Servings: 4

Ingredients:

- 1 Pineapple, cut into chunks
- 12 Strawberries, halved
- 2 Mangos, cut into chunks
- ½ cup Orange Juice
- 2 tbsp Honey
- 1 tbsp Brown Sugar
- 1 tbsp Butter

Method:

1. Preheat your grill to medium high.
2. Thread the fruit chunks onto soaked skewers.
3. Open the grill and place the skewers on the bottom grilling plate.
4. Cook for 3 minutes.
5. Flip over and cook for additional 3 minutes.
6. Meanwhile, combine the remaining ingredients in a small saucepan, and cook until slightly thickened.
7. Drizzle over the fruit skewers and serve. Enjoy!

Nutritional Value:

- Calories 180
- Total Fats 4g
- Carbs 22g
- Protein 2g
- Fiber: 1g

Apple Crips in Foil

Preparation Time: 15 minutes
Cooking Time: 20 minutes
Servings: 8

Ingredients:

- 4 Apples, sliced
- ½ cup Flour
- 4 tbsp Sugar
- 2 tsp Cinnamon
- ½ cup Quick Oats
- ½ cup Butter, melted
- ½ cup Brown Sugar
- ½ tsp Baking Powder

Method:

1. Preheat your grill to 350 degrees F.
2. Prepare 4 aluminium foil squares (about 8x12 inches each).
3. Divide the apple slices among the foil and sprinkle with sugar and cinnamon.
4. In a bowl, combine the remaining ingredients well.
5. Divide the mixture evenly among the foil packets.
6. Carefully foil the packets, sealing so the filling stays inside.
7. When ready, open the grill and unlock the hinge.
8. Lay the griddle grate on top of your counter and place the foils there.
9. Cook for about 10 minutes.
10. Then, flip over, and cook for 10 minutes more.
11. Carefully open the packets and let sit for about 10 minutes before consuming.
12. Enjoy!

Nutritional Value:

- Calories 318

- Total Fats 7g
- Carbs 51g
- Protein 2g
- Fiber: 3g

Coconut-Coated Pineapple

Preparation Time: 10 minutes
Cooking Time: 6 minutes
Servings: 6

Ingredients:

- 1 Pineapple
- 2 tbsp Honey
- 1 tbsp Coconut Cream
- 1/3 cup Shredded Coconut

Method:

1. Preheat your grill to medium high.
2. Meanwhile, peel and slice the coconut.
3. Thread each slice onto a soaked skewer.
4. Open the grill and arrange the skewers on top of the bottom plate.
5. Cook for 3 minutes per side.
6. Meanwhile, whisk together the honey and coconut cream.
7. Brush the pineapple with the mixture.
8. Place the coconut in a shallow bowl.
9. Coat the brushed pineapple with the coconut, on all sides.
10. Serve and enjoy!

Nutritional Value:

- Calories 75
- Total Fats 20g
- Carbs 20g
- Protein 0g
- Fiber: 1g

Grilled Peaches with Vanilla Ice Cream

Preparation Time: 10 minutes
Cooking Time: 6 minutes
Servings: 4

Ingredients:

- 4 Large Peaches
- 4 Scoops of Vanilla Ice Cream
- 2 tsp Honey
- 1 tbsp Butter, melted

Method:

1. Preheat your grill to medium high.
2. Cut the peaches in half and discard the pit.
3. Brush with butter on all sides, and place on top of the bottom grilling grate.
4. Cook for 3 minutes, then flip over, and cook for additional 3 minutes.
5. Transfer to a serving plate.
6. Wait a minute (so that your ice cream doesn't melt immediately), then drizzle with honey and add a scoop of ice cream on top.
7. Enjoy!

Nutritional Value:

- Calories 201
- Total Fats 4g
- Carbs 23g
- Protein 3g
- Fiber: 1g

Conclusion

I hope that this book was able to show you the perks of your amazing indoor appliance and enrich your recipe folder by 70 incredibly delicious recipes.

Now, the next step is pretty simple. Choose your favorite recipe, preheat your Hamilton Beach MultiGrill, and start grilling right away. Once you get the handle of this super-beneficial appliance, it will become your most reliable cooking weapon.

Whether breakfast, meat, or dessert, your HB 3-in-1 grill is here for you. Use this book to your advantage today!

Made in United States
Orlando, FL
23 November 2024

54322676R20059